T

OF THE
GREAT SUN

THE LIVES OF THE MICE IN OUR GARDEN

Best wishes

Julie x

THE TIME OF THE GREAT SUN

THE LIVES OF THE MICE IN OUR GARDEN

Julie A.D. Herrick

Holly Cottage Books

Time of the Great Sun
First published in Great Britain in 2022 by:
HOLLY COTTAGE BOOKS

Paperback ISBN 978-1-3999-0689-0

Book Published by:
HOLLY COTTAGE BOOKS

julieherrick@hotmail.com

Mumsie & Pa

"A mouse has a better chance of defeating a cat than a man competing against nature."

- Marty Rubin

CONTENTS

FOREWORD

My time of Lockdown was a mixed bunch of feelings, elation at not having to go to work, and sadness of not visiting, hugging, and kissing family members, being together with people and dancing too – and, so I looked to the wildlife in my garden. My partner and I spent so much time there as the weather was exceptional. We learnt about the funny ways the birds would communicate and perform around us, splashing about in the bird bath, taking their turn, and arguing too.

My partner loves to feed the birds and noticed one day, (as we sat in the sunshine), that the Dunnock's were getting left out. They seemed to just get the leftovers, shuffling around picking bits off the floor. One evening while out late the Dunnock's were seen in a very large plant pot, where grew an Acer tree. This gave my partner the idea for placing some food including meal worms and a small bowl of water there for them. Soon they found the food supply and we were happy they were getting fresh food. It wasn't long before the little Sparrows found out and a beautiful Robin. Mr. and Mrs. Blackbird came to feed their young close by too. There was a frenzy of arms-a-flapping when the Starlings sniffed them out, no way was my partner letting those greedy birds down to feed under the Acer - they had their own space. This happened a lot, it was quite funny to see... several times a day, I might add.

Then one day whilst looking through a pair of binoculars we spied the mice...

It's very peculiar how the make-up of stories can just pop into one's head; whether on a walk to the corner shop, in bed trying to sleep, or even driving (my partner taking notes). A story can stop and start until the next perspective or idea evolves and appears in written text.

This started as just one short story and slowly developed into something much bigger, and more exciting. It is mostly fiction, letting my imagination run with the feeling that every life form has a story to tell, and a life to live.

Along the way there will be many facts and there are some questions at the end for you to find the answers... in other books or the internet.

The Time of the Great Sun happens every year, but 2020 was different for everyone.

I do hope you enjoy this different twist on the Covid epidemic that devastated, and impacted on so many human lives.

But what of the animals? Did they notice?

Julie xx

THE SUN & THE MOON

We humans take for granted the rising and setting of the sun. We understand why the moon is in the sky at night, and we know where the sun, and moon are when we can't see them.

In the Summer the days feel so long, you can be out in the garden until 9 or 10pm and it's still light. We know Summer happens every year but mice only see one summer in their life time. For them, it is the time for having lots of babies, making friends, and restocking the store cupboard with food for the coming Winter.

As humans, we know the sun is a big ball of gas that has been burning for millions of years. Animals and humans need the sun to make plants and grasses grow. Flowers turn their faces to the sun to catch the rays, becoming seeds or fruit to eat. The animals call the Summer - The Time of the Great Sun - it is so big in the sky and lasts for such a long time every day. Throughout the history of mice, the word for Summer has changed only slightly, it has been a Big Sun, Long Light and Long Sun, finally they settled with the Great Sun.

The sun may go behind a cloud for a short while, and pop back out again; the warmth it gives is enjoyed so very much. It brightens our days, makes us smile and happy.

We can go on picnics, be outside, breathing in the joy of the Summer. The Great Sun can go behind a dark cloud and water we call rain will fall down from them. The rain can come as a very fine mist that will wet you like someone is spraying from a can, something like a hairspray. It can come as a steady flow, pitter pattering on your window, sliding down in tiny rivers, or come down in a heavy down pour. When the water gets very cold in the clouds, it can fall to the ground in lumps and hit the earth hard and fast. Sometimes it will turn into flakes of snow that will float down without a sound and cover the ground in a white soft blanket.

At night the sun goes to the other side of the world and shines on the southern hemisphere, for example a place called Australia. This is when we can see the Moon better – when it is dark. Sometimes it's small like a smile on its side and sometimes big and round like someone has switched on a torch, and found a hole in some black material. You can see the stars at night too. They are always there, even in the daytime but we cannot see them because the sun is so bright.

Stars twinkle and planets do not. The space station glides across the sky without a sound, and looks like it is being taken to the other side of the sky by a gentle breeze. Aeroplanes make a noise and you can see the red-light flashing from the tip of one of its wings.

Meteors/shooting stars do just that, shoot across the sky so very fast, you're not sure if you really did see it. Comet's travel fast too, but are so far away you can see them in the night sky for nearly a month at a time. They have a tail of burning rock trailing behind them!

When you see your first star or shooting star at night, make a wish, it may come true!

In the Winter the darkness lasts longer, we all get tucked in our homes and keep warm, with the fire burning and a hot chocolate drink in our hands, and a good movie on the TV.

The mice in this story call the Winter the - Long Darkness.

Many ‘light times’ and ‘short darkness’ are mentioned, meaning days and nights. Only humans have given these words to the passing of time.

What do you think mice do during The Time of the Great Sun? What do they think? Did they notice us in the garden more than usual?

I will pass the narration of the story over to Salta the mouse now, and you can read her story...

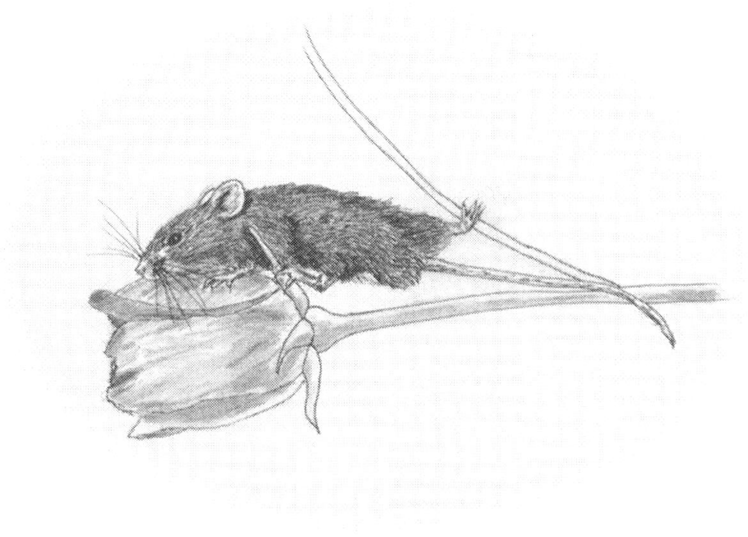

SALTA

Hi! My name is Salta, and I am a Wood Mouse. I was named after a comet that had been in the sky towards the end of the last Long Darkness. I had been born early as there had been mild weather, and my mother liked to look to the sky for inspirational names. Atlas, the comet's given name, was more a male name, so it was turned around and made into Salta. I am happy; I don't think I would like to be called Atlas.

I was born when the daffodils were just beginning to open their faces to the sun.

They sit there with their heads a bobbin' testing the temperature. Should they open, should they hide away a little longer?

When they open, they shout out their names and say hello to each other through their yellow trumpets. There's an outer fan around this, which is used to catch sound and direct it into the flower. I tell you; they can hear everything.

I lived with my family for some time until I was strong, could look after myself, and venture finally into the wildness beyond our family garden. I'd go a little further every darkness, and run back to my home, until my mother told me I must leave as she was due to have some more babies, that may be the last litter before she goes to sleep.

My brothers, sisters and myself, had all been shown how to find food and take care of ourselves. Many a time during the darkness we were told stories that had been passed down generation to generation. It was left to the females to remember and tell the stories because the males always left the nest and led their own lives.

We were told to take care during the darkness and fear the animals that would like to eat us for their dinner like foxes, snakes, weasels, hawks, owls, dogs and cats, and even toads will manage to eat a mouse if we pass by slowly! I might add here that we do have excellent hearing, which certainly helps in these scary situations; also we can run very fast, holding our tails high to help us balance.

We were told to stay indoors during the light and keep out of sight. Mother said the days of the Great Sun would soon be upon us when the light time was longer than the dark, there wouldn't be much time for food gathering.

The day I finally set off on my own was very sad but I was excited too. I had a short time to learn some more about life, what food to eat and how to make a nest. I learnt how to find my way around my space. Now you might wonder how we find our way back to our nests when we have been out... well, we are very clever and I am going to tell you something that may surprise you. As we are out on our travels, we will pick up objects, maybe a leaf or a twig and place them in a way only we can see and understand. These are the things that help guide us back home.

Soon it was time to find a male, and have lots of babies myself. I was looking forward to setting up home and becoming a Mummy Mouse. It was during one darkness I heard singing, such the sweetest song you ever did hear. I used my nose to sniff him out, and there sitting on a stone was a mouse who was very handsome.

What was most noticeable and bewitching, was the mop of curly hair he had on his head, it gave him a cute edge, that made me want to see and hear more. I sat for a while and listened, trying to keep out of sight. He was singing about a time when he hoped to meet a lady mouse whom he could love for the rest of his days. He wasn't going to be like the others and leave her to look after babies by herself.

Oh, I thought, this was my dream... Suddenly with all the excitement I moved slightly and made a noise.

Oops, my cover was blown!

He came over to me and said,

"I have seen you before, and wanted to get to know you. I knew this to be the path you travel. You have the most beautiful eyes, that doth catcheth the twinkling of the stars and the brightness of the moon," emphasising his words with expressive arms.

Ooh! I swooned, and cupped my front paws under my chin. As well as a good voice, he had a special way with words that just softened the soul.

His name is Dearest and I will tell you his story very soon.

We busied ourselves finding the perfect spot for our nest. Searching here and searching there. Until, it came to pass when we found the perfect spot. Idyllic, shaded by the most splendid shaped Acer I have ever seen. A garden of unrivaled proportions and interest... and a small amount of water in a container. I was so excited.

Dearest and I set about creating the best, most comfortable home, that was as close as possible to this garden. It wouldn't be too long before my babies arrived, so we scurried around fetching this and that, creating something I had only dreamed of.

I have a very good sense of smell and love hunting out my favourite seeds. I have to be busy, busy, busy, no time to rest. I'm afraid our lives are too short, there's way too much to fit in. I love to gossip, what mouse doesn't? On my travels to and fro I may pass another mouse or two and we will stop and have a chatter and maybe groom each other as a greeting. During the long darkness we may all live together (in a burrow with long tunnels under ground) to keep warm.

One darkness, I climbed a stick covered with thorns, right to the very top. The moon came a little closer, but I just couldn't reach it. I then heard a muffled voice. Where was it coming from? Oh, it was a flower bud, all wrapped up tightly. What was it saying? I got closer.

"You will like my petals for your nest. They are so delicately soft and have a lovely gentle perfume. They will keep your babies warm and relaxed, so they will sleep better."

"But where are your petals?" I asked.

"Come back soon and I will be ready," she replied.

After a few times of darkness, I excitedly returned, and what a beautiful sight, the flower was open.

"Hello young mouse," she said.

"Hello, my name is Salta."

"Hello Salta, have you come for some of my petals for your nest?"

"Oh, yes please, if that's alright?"

"Of course, I have many. Just bite a few off and take them home, you will be having your babies soon."

"Yes," I replied. "They are squirming and kicking around inside, a bit uncomfortable sometimes. My mother said there may be up to seven or eight in there!"

"Eight!" she exclaimed.

"I hope not, it's my first time," I explained.

So, I bit off one petal and carried it back to my nest, then went back for another.

"If you would like more, I have a sister on another stick who is willing to part with a few."

"Thank you... What is your name?" I asked.

"My name is Rose."

Dearest, I might add, did help to gather the petals. He is so sweet.

So, from then on, other mice could always tell it was me, as I wear the smallest rose you could possibly find tucked behind my ear. It also reminds me of the red tail of a comet burning its way across the sky.

Woops, it was time. My babies were born. There were only three, thank goodness. If all that jiff ling about was just for three, I don't like to think what eight will feel like!

Before I tell you about my lovely pink babies, I will introduce you to some other mice and animals I bump into now and again on my many wanderings.

DEAREST

As I've already announced, Dearest is the handsomest mouse I could have wished for, and he can sing and serenade better than any other. He was the only baby to be born to his mother at a similar time to me, and she loved him so very much, such a dear sweet thing, Dearest was the only possible name he could be given.

Their nest was not too far from ours I believe... well he has explained to me, we were nearly neighbours. Anyway, without my knowledge, he had noticed me, it's surprising what goes on without us realising, isn't it?

His mother instilled in him thoroughly good manners. Saying “please” and “thank you,” and “how are you?” Dearest can speak to most animals about almost anything, enjoys conversation, will help out and take care of his loved ones. Because he was the only mouse born for the last pregnancy of his mother, he always had an extra special place in her heart and she wanted him to do well in his life. He was encouraged to ask the ‘How’s’, the ‘Where’s’ and the ‘Why’s’... as this is the only way to find out things, and learn. It was also approved for him to go wandering to experience new things. He would go home to his mother and relay his findings, who would sit and listen with interest.

He tells me tales of his adventures; far more than I had I might add. Once he found himself in a place that was full of tall plants, with yellow flowers right at the very top. The flowers swayed in the breeze and dropped powder on him as he passed, and he found himself sneezing.

"We like to make you sneeze," sneered the flowers. "Every life form sneeze's or has runny eyes and nose's. We think it's funny," they all laughed.

"Hey you, yellow flower, what's your name?" he shouted.

"Ha, Ha. We are called Brassica," taunted the flowers, and they carried on smiling and watching him in a funny sort of way.

As he looked up to say he certainly wouldn't be travelling this way again, a Bee flew by and disappeared into one of the flowers. Dearest wondered what was happening, why could he now only see the Bee's bum?

It was in there a while, and Dearest was mesmerised, as he could see the bee collecting the same yellow powder that had made him sneeze, and placing it on its back legs.

The Bee then left the flower and flew to another, to do the same again! But as it backed out some of the yellow powder fell on Dearest, and oh, he sneezed again!

"What is that Bee doing?" he mumbled shaking his fur and trying not to breath too deeply.

Miss Bee heard the question and buzz, buzz buzzed down to see Dearest.

"Wouldzz youzz likezz to knowzz?"

"Oh yes please."

"Well, I takez zzizz polenzz backz to myzz homezz, an' weez makzz it intozz honeyzz for foodzz in zze cold timezz. I canzz bring youzz some to tryzz if youzz likzz."

"That would be very kind of you Miss Bee, thank you."

Miss Bee said her Goodbyezzz and continued her task.

As Dearest turned to head home a beetle landed near him, "Oh dear, oh dear," she cried. "I must go find Little Ann."… She huffed and puffed, opened her cape, stretched out her wings and flew away. Dearest just had enough time to call after her "I h-hope you find her." He was left there staring, watching the beetle get smaller and smaller.

After some time had passed, Miss Bee came to Dearest's home and brought him a little present of some honey. He called a few of his friends to join him and they enjoyed a lovely sweet feast together.

I wouldn't say he is overly brave, but inquisitive. Not as brave as a Blackbird is, when faced with a large family of Starlings all fighting for the same food, but in this next adventure you will hear that he certainly has a go at being brave, if needs must.

One time while he was out and about, water began to fall from the sky in big drops. Every now and again one would land on him and make a big splashing sound. Luckily his fur is silky smooth and doesn't let the water in, so each drop slid off very quickly.

He was late for a gathering, when a story of the ancestors would be related, and he came to some water that he couldn't be bothered to go around. He looked about, and there was a large leaf nestled nearby. He wondered if he stood on it, would the wind take him to the other side?

So, on he stepped.

Woo, the wind played with the leaf, moving it this way and that way. Dearest held on only to find he was back where he had started. Not wanting to chance his luck again, he jumped off and ran as quickly as he could around the water and back to his home, arriving just in time for the story, but breathing very fast, so much so the rest of the mice wondered where he had been and what he had been up to!

As you know we met one darkness, and have been together ever since. Mice don't usually do this, but Dearest wanted to look after me and take care of all the babies we were going to have.

KES

Now Kes he came from quite a distance. We know not from where, and nor does he, but he has been welcomed into our local group of mice. He is a little older than me.

He is very brave and determined, and I might add, loves to tell tales and stories. He can turn any short event into a dramatic and enthusiastic crowd pleaser. The way he delves into the depth of feelings and excitement, you truly can be absorbed, and live in his words. He has one of those voices that you just have to listen to. I do sometimes wonder if he colours in the gaps of his adventures, but I would never confront him with these questions.

And there he is... I have just spotted him. You can tell its him as he only has one ear, poor Kes. Let us join him for his most famous of tales. The – 'How' and 'Why', he has a scar on his back. There is always a mixture of ages in the audience of mice. They have all congregated in a small clearing under some conifer trees.

"Gather round," he says.

"Gather round. For I will tell you the tale of the great bird. A bird of the greatest agility and stealth.

"I was only a little younger than I am at the moment, when I ventured into a place of the full sky. The Great Sun shone and there were no shadows, the ground felt dry and hot under my paws and the grass smelt warm. I suppose you may ask what does warm smell like? But when you smell it, you will know.

"Anyway, I was wandering around minding my own business, searching out all the different type of grasses I had been told about, learning to recognise the ones that produce good seed to eat, and also to store away - when suddenly my mind did a back flip.

“Had I wandered too far away from my family?

“My intrigue and lust for knowledge had led me astray. I said to myself... I must aim to find my way home... As you know, we mice can travel quite a distance, mostly in the darkness, but this was during the time the Great Sun was high in the sky. I turned and tried to retrace my steps, but I had been foolish and not made the signs on the ground to help me return safely. What was I to do?

“All of a sudden the Great Sun turned dark, a shadow appeared over me, a flapping sinister shadow. I then felt this chill surge through my bones and I was unable to move. I was stuck fast, my heart beat louder and my eyes widened. My whole-body shook, and I moved. This I had been warned, this I had been told repeatedly not to do.

Do not move or you will be seen. Truly I only moved slightly, I'm sure I only moved slightly…

"In a flash - a breeze hit me as a bird dropped vertically, and swooped me up in his talons. Sharp, yellow claws wrapped round me, I hung there, rising higher and higher off the ground.

"I must admit it's quite fascinating how the shortest of moments seem to last so very long in a situation like that.

"But, where was I going? The bird's belly feathers moved and parted in the wind, its wings beat so steadily and rhythmically, it was quite mesmerising. I must not be lured in by the pulse I thought... Con-cen-trate...

"I shouted out as loud as I could, WHERE ARE YOU TAKING ME?

“He answered in a high-pitched screeching giggle…

“ ‘My dear Fal-con
is si-tting up-on her eggs,
and she is very hun-gry...
You were in the wrong place,
at the wrong time.
Now you are her din-ner.’ ”

“Oh dear, thought I. I was heading towards a nest, what was I to do?”

"WRIGGLE KES, WRIGGLE." The mice had heard this story many a time, and all answered with loud eagerness.

"Yes, so I started to wriggle and wriggle, those talons where tight around me, but, and I do not know to this day why, but, my continuous squirming and moving about had set me......"

"Frreeeeeeeee," the mice sang. Sometimes they try to see who can make it last the longest, and end out of breath and laughing with joy.

"Oh no, I was falling, falling so very fast towards the ground. From just above the trees to the ground is such a long way for a little mouse like me. I had escaped being food for an incubating falcon, but what harm would a fall cause me? Was I staring death in the face again? Umph!!! Umph!! Umph!" he said, and the others joined in...

"I had landed... my lungs had been emptied of air... but yes, I was still alive."

"HURRAY," the audience cheered with glee.

"I took a big deep breath and looked around me... Where was I?"

“YOU WERE HERE,” shouted the eagerly listening mice.

“Yes I was, and I had landed on a long soft thing, just the other side of your garden Salta. Didn’t I?” he asked. (I nodded as I sat behind all the other mice.)

“Through all that, I didn’t know I had been hurt. The bird had caught my back, I was bleeding. My dear Salta there, (he pointed to me) took me in. A stranger. Took me in and cared for me, made me better. But I have this scar here,” he pointed to his left side.

“I have this scar to remind me to never go out into the open on my own or to forget the ways of mice and remember to leave a trail of signs. I have learnt from doing wrong, you young mice must learn from me. I have since been told that I was very lucky as usually the bird, which we know as a Kestrel... and dear Salta gave me my name,” he smiled, “usually bites their captured prey as soon as it is caught! I was so lucky on that day, as I only lost my ear as you can see. I came here and have a new family with all of you. I am so happy.”

All the mice shouted and cheered and gathered around, and said they were pleased too that Kes had arrived, as they never tired of his story of the bird. They had learned a very important lesson too.

LITTLE LYCHEE

Oh Lychee, I must tell you of Lychee. A little younger than myself but full of words and very outspoken. She knows her own mind, knows what she wants and goes out and takes it with all the gusto she can manage.

I found her one darkness seated under a flower. A flower I might add that was very highly perfumed. So perfumed I was confused as to whether it was a fruit of some kind. My mother tried to describe the fruits I could eat by the scent being sweet and a description of what they would look like. But here was a flower that held all of the different fruit scents, all at the same time.

This little mouse was taken by the fragrance and just sat there, dreamily beneath the stars and inhaled deeply.

"Hello," I said.

"Oh hello, isn't it just divine, the smell of this flower? Her name is Madame Pierre, don't you think it's a lovely name?"

"It certainly is," I agreed. "I came here as I thought there was some fruit ready to be eaten, but I thought it a little early for them really."

"Yes, but this smell is strong enough to imagine you are eating fruit."

"You would need a good imagination if your tummy was empty but yes, it is yummy."

"Oh, my tummy isn't empty, I've just had my fill of cheese."

"But mice don't like cheese."

"Oh, I do, and there's always plenty of it," she replied.

"Where do you find this cheese?" I enquired.

"Oh, over in that place of wood. Some 'Beings'," she lowered her voice, "go in there now and again. They keep big metal things in there and a bag of bird seed that I opened one time. The seed came running out, escaping from being confined, I took some home to my family."

"You must be careful, the 'Beings' there have been known in the past to put out traps for mice. They kill us just because we are hungry," I exclaimed.

"Ha ha, yes I know I have seen them. I don't think the 'Beings' like me to be there getting seed. I have seen their traps. They put cheese on them. Silly, they think mice like cheese for some reason. Most of the time the traps are left and more seed is taken ha ha," she chuckled.

"You are very brave to go there."

"Oh it's fine... and I have taken a liking to the cheese," she smiled confidently.

"Oh," I gasped. "Surely not, but how... how?... and you are still alive?"

"It's easy, they are not very good traps and if you approach from the right angle, up, up and awaaaay!" she cried.

Oh dear I felt this mouse was dicing with death, but she seemed so sure and brave. She was certainly no ordinary mouse.

"Do not worry," she fearlessly stated. "What is your name?"

"My name is Salta, named after the great comet seen in the sky."

"I haven't been given a name yet, my family are still thinking," she said sulkily.

"Well, you like cheese...why not Lychee?"

"Now that is a cool name. Lychee, yes, I like that. Thank you Salta."

"No problem, I think it suits you. What do you have around your wrist?" I had noticed very small lumps of something, threaded together by a thin piece of grass.

"Oh, oh oh," she giggled. "Spare pieces of cheese of course.

"Of course Lychee, of course," I sighed with a knowing smile.

She grinned, shrugged her shoulders and said she ought to be off, and hoped we would see each other again very soon.

"Yes, that would be nice... but take care, won't you?"

"Of course, do not fear," she shouted as she took off in the direction of the wooden place.

I busied myself hunting a few morsels of food, looking under leaves and twigs, when all of a sudden Lychee raced by carrying a piece of cheese, her head lifted high so as to not trip over the prize lump between her teeth. Her tail was raised in excitement too.

"Hi Hal-ha," she cheered as she struggled to say my name with her mouth full!

I shook my head and mumbled to myself that the 'Beings' would be annoyed again when they found an empty trap!

So, there's Lychee, the daredevil of the mouse world. We call her Little Lychee because she is sweet and small... but doesn't know we call her 'Little'... don't tell her, will you?!!

THE BEINGS

Well, the main story of this book is about the 'Beings', and, as they have just been mentioned, I ought to explain something about them…

As you already know Dearest and I found a lovely place to live, and our piece of garden had a beautiful Acer tree growing there.

Fresh water always available and most importantly, food. I believe it was put there especially for Prunella and her friends (I'll explain later) but Dearest and I found the food too. Mealworms, and they were lovely. We peered through the bricks... our little noses sniffing the air and the beautiful aroma of the meal worms.

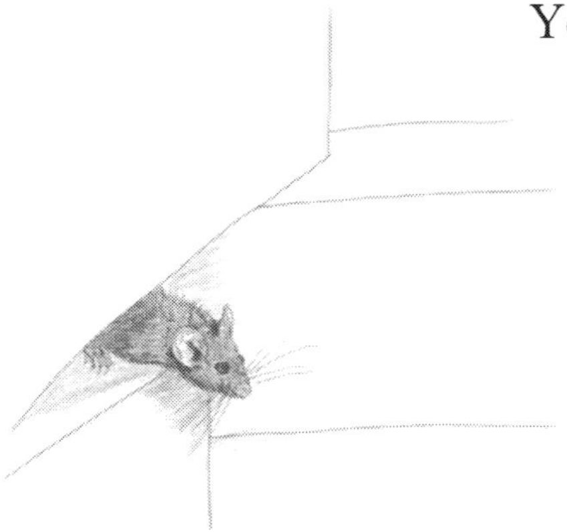

Was it safe to go out? Yes quickly, quickly... Oh no birds! They would come and scare us or we would make them fly away.

Eventually, after some time we sat side by side with both the Dunnocks including Prunella, and Mr & Mrs Sparrow eating the same food. It took a little while to get used to each other, but it was lovely to be able to do this.

The food appeared exactly the same time the sun reached the top of the Acer tree.

Once we were a little early and we saw, to our amazement, a bald 'Being' arrive, shaking something. It sounded like something rough and dry. Dearest and I stayed back, hid and watched. The 'Being' spread the mealworms out onto our garden and refreshed the water in our little container. Dearest and I looked at each other, this was amazing we were so lucky, now we knew. Now we knew where all the food was coming from.

There are two 'Beings'. One I believe to be male, the bald one, and the other... a female. They are the life forms in the space just beyond our garden.

The female sits surrounded by sticks of wood, so close to us.

She looks at flapping sheets with pictures on them, and quietly watches us, but we saw her first. We were watching her, watching us.

The bald 'Being' sits further away holding things against his face that shine sometimes like the Great Sun.

We seem to be their entertainment.

Cody (a mouse friend of ours) shows off sometimes climbing the bricks near the Acer, pulling food up and over them, as once they gave us a big crust of something. I wanted to break it up into smaller pieces to be able to take it back home easily, but no... Cody wanted to do it all at once. He struggled, pulling it this way and that way. Huffing and puffing. Pushing it. Pushing it up a brick towards a waiting Lychee, who pulled it up with all her might. They got there in the end but I'm sure it could have been achieved with a lot less effort.

Myself and other mice have noted that the 'Beings' seem to be about more often, spending so much time in the space beyond our garden. They always seem to be there, though throughout our history, this has rarely happened, which was strange. Why was this? We were all a little confused. Carrying on with our tasks we kept an eye on the situation, and hoped to find out the reason.

CODY

Cody, dear Cody. He is only a little younger than me and what a cheeky mouse he is, but not very daring I might add. He pushes others forward to do certain deeds, while he stays behind and then acts big, as if it was his idea and he has done all the hard work, if, and a big if, all goes to plan. I'm sure everyone knows someone like this.

Even so, he has the spirit and twinkle in his eye that just makes you forgive and hug him.

I met him one darkness when he was racing around playing hide and seek.

"Hey you mouse, I bet you can't find me?"

"My name isn't Hey you, IT'S SALTA," I shouted after him.

He disappeared, soon followed by other mice. "Which way did he go? Which way did he go?" they all called. Me being me I pointed in the wrong direction and smiled to myself.

I continued my journey looking for seeds and acknowledging other mice along my route when all of a sudden, out of breath, Cody appeared before me. "Where did they all go?" he puffed.

"I sent them the other way, was that the right thing to do?"

"Thank you, Salta, it gives me a breather from my young cousins, they always want to play hide and seek. I caught them out the other day and hid in that old bird's nest up there," he pointed up into a tree. "There were some old feathers in it, they were lovely and soft. I laid stroking them and fell asleep. They found me all curled up, and said I was the worst mouse to play hide and seek with," he laughed, "but they always come back to me to play."

Cody is one of those mice that brings joy and happiness into our lives, and if we miss seeing him during the darkness or, for that matter when the Great Sun is there smiling, I, and I know others miss his little face and the tuft of hair on his head that will just not lay down.

Once he found a pile of grass cuttings and hid. I was told that he kept making passing mice jump as he suddenly appeared with a cry of "A-ha," and sprayed grass all around. The mice said they were either scared and ran off as fast as they could, or looked and saw Cody with grass balancing on his head like a hat, and laughed at his antics.

Then there was the time he planned an expedition with a few of his younger friends and cousins. He had noticed a plant growing up the side of a wall. Next to the plant was a white square where the sky could be seen. He was amazed that the sky could be seen in two places at the same time. They were to climb the plant and see what was different about the sky in this square. It was Cody's idea but of course he sent one of the youngest up there first. He wasn't going to test it out and fall into the sky.

So up his little cousin went encouraged greatly by Cody and the others. The poor thing climbed higher and higher.

There were some big flowers ready to open.

"What are you doing here young mouse? There's nothing up here for you today."

"I've been told to come up here to see the sky."

"Do you always do everything you are told young mouse?"

"Er no?"

"I should think not, it can be very dangerous, you must think first before agreeing to do things."

"I am a bit scared about falling into the sky," said the young mouse with a quivering little voice.

"Sky?... that's not the sky, it's a reflection of the sky in a window. The only place you will fall is down to the ground if you don't hold on tight," the flower explained.

The mouse climbed down the plant and told Cody that it was just a re-flec-tion of the sky and wasn't real. "I knew that," said Cody.

With this knowledge Cody went up the plant, now knowing he couldn't fall into the sky, and got a big shock when a 'Beings' face appeared at the window.

“Arrrgh,” cried Cody and scrambled down as fast as he could.

“What's wrong Cody?” the mice waiting for him exclaimed.

“Nothing, nothing is wrong. I’ve just realised we are late for dinner.” Cody did go back to see if the ‘Being’ would be there again, he was inquisitive, but it never appeared at the window. The flower asked him what he was looking for?

“There was a ‘Beings’ face at that window, I saw it.”

“Yes,” said the flower, “for some reason, not at this moment in time.”

“Is it the same ‘Being’ that feeds us?”

“Yes,” said the flower, “feeds and waters me too.”

“What is your name?” asked Cody.

“My name is Nelly Moser,” she replied.

Cody thanked Nelly for her help and said he would go and see her again soon.

RAPUNZ

Rapunz is a good friend of Dearest. They go about for food together, sit, talk, and discuss the ways of mice and other animals. He is wise because he always knows the right questions to ask. I have learnt many things through his talks with Dearest, for example the names of birds and how to tell them apart.

Oh dear, but poor Rapunz has a problem. He is different to the rest of the mice... he has extra-long hair! It makes him look wild and windblown, but we know him to be caring and lovely. His mother was most confused when his hair wouldn't stop growing, and we still don't know why. I saw him rushing a little too fast one darkness, when all of a sudden, he stepped on his hair and over he went, into a roly poly. He came to a halt, sat up and stared straight ahead in a bit of a daze. He then saw me as he peered out behind his long hair, our eyes met, and a big grin came upon his face. We both laughed and laughed so much, our tummy's hurt. He gets used to this though, he has done it sooo many times.

He is always laughing, such a happy mouse, but... he has a small piece of his tail missing! Here is his tale... sorry I couldn't help that little joke.

It was story time for the little mice and they all gathered around. Some sat on a mushroom, giving them height to see Rapunz over the heads of the other mice. Once seated comfortably, Rapunz began.

"One darkness I was out and about, minding my own business," he explained. "When the scent of a cat drifted past my nose." He wafted a paw in front of his face. The young ones gasped and the older ones joined in. They had heard it all before, but they liked to help bring drama to the occasion.

"My hair stood on end," he grinned, and held his hair up with his front paws... "As best as it could," he added with a cheeky sigh.

"What was I to do?"

"RUN!" was shouted out.

"I most certainly did run, but do you know what happened next?"

"YOU FELL OVER YOUR HAIR," shouted Cody from the back. He always has to add this piece of information. All the mice turned round to look at him, and then quickly back to Rapunz.

"Yes, I fell over my hair," he continued. "Down I fell, lost valuable moments, and the cat caught me up!

"Oh dear, oh dear... I scrambled up and started to run again, just-as-the-naughty-cat picked me up by my tail! Up, up, up I went in to the air. I wriggled and wriggled, my paws beating the air as fast as they could."

“What happened then Rapunz?” squeaked a little mouse.

“THE END OF HIS TAIL FELL OFF,” yelled out Cody.

"Cody do you always have to spoil the ending?" reprimanded Rapunz.

"Sorry," he bashfully replied. Poor Cody, he does get so excited.

"Cody is correct, the end of my tail came off and I fell to the ground and ran as fast as I could. The cat stood in wonderment, holding a small piece of my tail in its mouth. I had been very lucky, very lucky indeed.

"So little mice, what should you do if you get caught by your tail? He looked up and Cody was just about to shout out the answer. Rapunz held up one paw."

"No Cody… leave it to one of the other mice to answer this time," Cody relaxed his shoulders and sighed.

"Wriggle, wriggle, wriggle," wriggled the same little mouse in the front row who had asked the question earlier, but for some reason hadn't been given a name. He had been listening with wide eyes in wonderment.

"Yes, correct young mouse. Yes, you must wriggle. Wriggle like... shall we call you

Wriggle young mouse?" Rapunz asked with pleasure in his eyes.

All the mice cheered, and said that would be a very good name, and so Wriggle came to be. He was very happy and proud to be named. He was patted on the back by all in attendance.

"Tails probably won't grow back," Rapunz picked up his own stubby tail, "but this is a most useful thing to happen, and I was very pleased for the chance to live again. So be very careful."

If you ever find a mouse with a shorter tail than another, you now know why.

MR TOAD

Mr Toad, is a grumpy old Toad. He sits and waits, sits and waits, camouflaged so well against the dry leaves and earth. He crawls around with an ungainly plod, huffing and puffing with such an effort.

He likes to eat woodlice, slugs, beetles, caterpillars, flies, and earthworms. He seems very slow when he wanders around, then sits with his eyes closed - but he is just pretending… I know. He has a very, very quick sticky tongue that can catch even a mouse unawares and eat them!

Dearest and I wondered if he might know about the 'Beings', so we headed out one darkness to find him. We found him, but kept our distance of course.

"Hey Toady, how you doing?" Dearest said with the most cheerful voice, trying not to show any fear.

Toady opened his eyes with slow sophistication, showing he really didn't want to talk. After a while he spoke very slow and precisely.

"You're being very brave young mouse. I haven't managed to catch a mouse for quite a while, nearly forgetting what you taste of," he looked in our direction and burped! Dearest and I grinned at each other and, showing respect didn't comment.

"Oh Toady, we will not come any closer than this, we know you have a long tongue," Dearest replied.

"To answer your question, I am very well thank you, and my name is Buffer" he burped again! Dearest muffled a giggle.

"Oh Buffer... Why Buffer?" I asked.

"Oh, there are two of you. A very tasty meal you both would make," he said, and burped!

Dearest was trying his hardest not to laugh out loud, I kept having to nudge him, "Stop it," I whispered.

"At one time we were considered the same as those lively jumping frogs, but thankfully it was decided we were **not** the same! *Burp, Burp*!... The scientific name for a Toad is Bufo bufo, and frogs have been given Rana... *Burp*... I know this because in the past Toads used to work alongside those 'Beings' you see about."

"My name is Salta and this is Dearest. Have you always lived around here?"

"I came from that big pond over there, at least three Great Suns ago. I started life as a little thing like a fish – called a tadpole, and, as if by magic, my tail disappeared, I grew legs and here I am, a Toad. *Burp*!"

"Wow," exclaimed Dearest. "That is truly magical."

He puffed himself up and made himself look a lot bigger. He was a proud Toad. (Although I have been told since, they do this to attempt to look bigger, and ward off anything that may eat them!)

"Aha, yes. A Toad's ancestry is in magic, did you know? *Burrrrp*!"

"No," I smiled. Dearest was now hiding behind me shaking with the effort not to laugh.

"Yes, we used to help Witch's... 'Beings' with pointed black heads, by spying on their enemies. We were very good at it. *Burp*. There are no Witch's around here though, and so I do not have a job. *Burp*!"

"Buffer, do you know why there are so many 'Beings' about, we have noticed there are more about than usual?"

"No, and I don't.... *BBUUURRRRPPPPP*" Wow, he did the biggest burp e-vverrrr! The leaves rustled and Dearest's little curl's on the top of his head quivered with surprise.

With that, Dearest burst out laughing and made me jump. He must have scared Buffer as well, as he raised himself up on all four limbs and looked so very frightening, we ran away as fast as we could. Giggling as we took our escape.

WHAT IS THIS LITTLE BEETLE?

Dearest had told me about meeting a beetle while he was out and about once. I looked and looked to find one myself, then, while exploring around under some wood, I suddenly came upon two perfectly smooth rounded shapes. They were I'm sure, sunning themselves. The light from the Great Sun hit their spotted domed backs and dazzled me slightly. The spots were most unusual.

I approached them gingerly and sniffed. They had a peculiar odour, I cannot quite describe.

There was no sign of legs, head or even a tail like mine, but I could hear something. Was it a conversation? Their voices were quite high and they spoke very fast, it took me a while to understand.

"......oh I know Neli dear."

"But what do you think C?"

"I don't think anything Neli dear, its just a pity that's all I can say."

"Mmm."

"Neli dear we are being watched."

"I saw it coming behind you, I've already started my Reflex Blood."

"Oh, Neli dear you could have told me."

"You'll be safe with me C."

I didn't want to scare them, so I softly said "Hello."

"Oh, it speaks, it speaks Neli dear!"

"Yes C, just stay quiet and it might go away."

“My name is Salta; you have the loveliest shiny backs I have ever seen.” I hoped a little courtesy may help the situation.

“Is it talking to you C, or to me?”

“I don’t know Neli dear, but it seems friendly.”

“Mmm.”

I looked around them “Do you have legs and a tail? I asked.

“If you must know we do, we do.”

“We most certainly do, do, do,”

“But we don’t have a tail, no no, we don’t have a tail. That would be funny wouldn’t it Neli dear?”

“Mmm.”

“I love the spots on your backs, why do you have spots?” I inquired.

“Spots, spots?”

“You have spots C.”

“Neli dear you have spots, but I didn’t know I had spots.”

“Yes C, you most certainly do, do, do.”

“Why do we have spots Neli dear?”

"To stop things eating us C, to stop things eating us."

"Yes Neli and you switched on your Reflex Blood too, to ward off attackers."

"Mmm."

"You are so sweet both of you, what are your names?" I asked politely.

"This is Neli and I am C."

"Yes C, but it, I mean Salta, might want to know our full names not the names we call each other as friends."

"Of course, Neli dear, of course."

"My name is Neliday and this is Coci."

"Hello to you both. You have very nice names," I praised.

"Oh thank you, thank you" replied Neliday.

"And you are a mouse?" asked Coci.

"Yes Coci, I have been wandering around this pile of wood to find food," I explained.

"Mmm," said Neliday.

"You have seven spots on your back," I looked from one to the other. "You both have."

"Ah ha, you will have seven children in your next litter," exclaimed Neliday.

"That will be nice, I only had three in my first. That's good to know. I can prepare myself," I smiled.

"We will lay many eggs, near where we know there will be food for them."

"You do not feed them yourself?" I asked.

"Oh no, no, no," Neliday exclaimed. "They can feed themselves as soon as they hatch. No, no, no we have other things to do."

"If we know there's no food about, we can delay laying our eggs until there is," explained Coci.

"That's very clever," I nodded.

"Mmm," said Neliday.

"What do you eat?" I asked "Surely not seeds and meal worms like me?"

"Oh no, no, no. No, we eat much smaller bugs than ourselves, called Aphids," explained Neliday.

"Aphids suck the sap from plants which is not very good for them, the plants that is. The 'Beings' are not very happy about this so they like having us in their gardens, helping them care for their plants eating the bugs," explained Coci.

"Talking of the 'Beings', they are in their gardens all the time, do you know why?" I asked.

"No dear no, we don't have time to ask questions, too much to do, too much to do," Neliday quickly answered.

"I have a question for you Neliday. I've been told there are beetles like you with only 2 spots, are they babies?"

"Oh no no, no, they are different Ladybirds to us."

"La-dy-bird, what a lovely name. It's a very soft and smooth sounding name, suits you I must say."

"I'm thinking about food now, Neli dear," Coci sounded eager to be away.

"Yes yes, yes, we must go C."

With that they stood up! Oh oh, they did have legs. One, two, m, m, m, six! Their capes opened. One then the other, stretching up and out to either side. Most beautiful. Then, I couldn't believe my eyes. Out came two gorgeous, thin, see-through wings, that shone all different colours, (well as many as I, a mouse can see) and unfolded so gracefully. I was amazed where and how they kept them. It seemed the two sides of the cape were their front wings.

They were very neat little beetles.

With that they both cried "Find Ann!" and left the floor with incredible style, poise, and, without a sound, flew off.

I sat staring up at them, their little legs dangling free. They left me very curiously wondering why they call that out when they fly off. "Find Ann." Dearest had told me this too. Next time I meet one of these beetles I must ask them...

BIG BUZZY THING

Dearest met a Big Buzzy Thing that flew very close to the ground. Hovering around going away and coming back again, looking a little lost.

I will let Dearest tell you this story, he is excited to have his speech written down. Please note he puts on his best voice - I have to chuckle to myself.

Here he is by some stones, some very small stones. Mice are actively congregating, knowing there will be a story told very soon.

"Ahem, gather round one and all, gather round, for I will tell you the time I met a Big Buzzy Thing," he said, proudly addressing his audience.

(Quite a gathering I must say, as a lot of mice are wondering what a Big Buzzy Thing is)

"I found a Big Buzzy Thing that looked decidedly lost. Are you lost Big Buzzy Thing? I asked. There was no reply. I SAY... I shouted, ARE YOU LOST?

"'MMMMMMmmmmmmmmmmmmmmm' it said,

"ARE ...YOU.... LOST? I repeated loudly. It didn't answer me, I thought it most rude. But then it passed me and landed on the ground.

"'Sorry dear mouse was you talking to me?' it said in a *very* posh voice. I realised then, it was a lady Buzzy Thing... I hope you like my voice; I am trying to be the posh Buzzy Lady.

(The young Mice were silent, just taking it all in.)

"'I cannot hear a blessed thing dear, not a thing. I can only sense vibrations. Vibration's dear that is all, so if you have a question, I cannot answer you. But I can give you my short lecture. My short lecture I give everyone, and hope the question you want answering, is in there somewhere.'

"I thought, I may-as-well listen to what she has to say

"'I slept in a hole dear over the Long Darkness, and was just about ready to wake up when I was dug out. Yes, dug out. I was thrown out of my house by a 'Being'. My hole in the ground was then covered by these stones you see here, and I keep forgetting. I keep forgetting and coming back, looking around for my house, then I remember it has gone. I have another one now. I have laid my eggs and I am now busy collecting pollen, no good waiting for the men to do it. They don't collect pollen, it's down to us girls to do it!'

"At this point I looked at her and wondered how she flew; her body was so big compared to her little wings. Then looked at myself. If I had wing's they would have to be...

'gi-norm-in-ous'.

"'Ha I see you looking at me like that, I can tell you are wondering how I fly. You do not even need to ask the question. I don't know either dear. Not at all, no. All I do know is I flap my wings very, very fast and up I go. I flap them so fast I make lots of heat so I can be the first out and last in of all the insects who collect pollen. Isn't that clever Hummmmm?'

"I gave her a big nod of my head to let her know I had understood her and smiled. I hoped my smile looked friendly because it was.

"'Dear mouse I must get on' she said. 'I have my pollen baskets with me to fill, we don't keep large amounts of honey like those other bees. We have to keep going out and about, out and about, always having a fresh stock, so to speak. That's when it can be bad for us you see. If there aren't many flowers, we run out of food dear. Yes, run out of food. I do hope I have told you everything you need to know, it's so difficult having no ears like you. Anyway, I'll get going, I might see you around, but don't think I'm ignoring you. Bye for now.'

"'MMMMMMmmmmmmmmmmmmmmm'

"I'm good at the MMmmmmmm sound, aren't I?"

(I had to smile, he looked so pleased with himself.)

"And she flew up and away, looking a bit wobbly at first until she got going properly. I was amazed, such a nice lady, very gentle and fluffy.

"So there you are young mice my story of the Big Buzzy Thing."

"But what was the Big Buzzy Thing called?" shouted a mouse from the back.

"Erm."

(Poor Dearest looked bashful)

"Erm, I didn't ask, and of course she didn't tell me, because she couldn't hear me anyway. Oh dear I hope I see her again."

All the mice said that it didn't matter, they still enjoyed the story and they would look out for a Big Buzzy thing that had wings smaller than its body.

I congratulated Dearest on his presentation and different voices. Of course, we went home and celebrated.

WINNIPEG

Winni is a hedgehog, who has so far lived for three Great Suns. Her house is quite close to ours, and she passes by every night on her hunt for something squidgy to eat. She is very motherly, and likes to know that we are all well and happy. She had some babies last Great Sun and is hoping to find a male to make some more.

Winni will love it if there's more than one that comes to visit, as there'll be much commotion, head-butting and chasing around until the best one wins, and Winni will smile her biggest smile.

Hedgehogs have prickly backs. They are very sharp, and Winni, I must tell you this, Winni always carries some of her bedding around with her. I don't think other hedgehogs do but she does. Sometimes it is some dried leaves, sometimes little sticks, and once I saw her with a few feathers caught. Just those tiny fluffy down feathers that sit and waft and wave unbeknown to the host. We never tell her; we smile, and some muffle a giggle if she is talking and the little feathers are waving to us in the breeze.

Oh, look here is Winni, telling her story, she has picked a lovely place. I can see Rose, Madame Pierre, and I can hear the sound of water sprinkling into a very large expanse of water. Let's go and listen, she is just starting.

"When I was young, I had a mishap one short darkness. So much pain in one of my legs. Awww I had walked as far as I could, until I could walk no more, I had to lay down.

"I lay very still until the Great Sun appeared and shone brightly, as what else could I do?" she sighed. "When suddenly I felt, in the ground, pounding vibrations. Oh no I thought, and squeezed my eyes tight shut and rolled myself up as tight as I could. The sounds were 'Beings' I just knew. What were they going to do?"

"Pick you up, pick you up," shouted a very excited Little Lychee, jumping up and down.

"Yes Lychee, I rose up and up. I flew like a bird, no word of a lie, I flew like a bird.

"I soared high without weight," Winni always chuckles here. "I will never feel as light as I did then, as you know I try and eat at least 100 creepy crawlies every darkness."

"What do you eat?" asked Rapunz, he already knew the answers, as he had enquired when the story had been told previously, but he was asking this time just in case the younger mice didn't know. He believes the only way to learn is to ask questions.

"I eat worms, beetles, slugs, caterpillars, earwigs, millipedes and leatherjackets. I do eat mice”... screams from Cody at the back!... “Buuutt only if I find a dead one.”

The loudest sigh came from Little Lychee who seemed to want to outdo Cody for some reason.

“Le-th-jack-ets? What are they?” questioned Wriggle.

“They are caterpillar type things but they turn into daddy-long-legs. You will see them later when the Great Sun doesn’t reach so high in the sky. They are rather scrummy. I try not to eat with my mouth open, but I do make a noise somewhat!” she laughed.

“Anyway, shall I get back to my story?’

“Yeeeees,” the mice cried.

“Well, I flew into a warm place, given plenty of food, and nice clean bedding. The next time I woke I had a stick stuck to my leg!”

“A stiiiiick?”

A chorus of mice was heard singing this word. Starting high, going low, high again, then they all giggled together.

“Yes, a stick, I tried to shake it off but it was stuck fast, and really I couldn’t move my leg anyway!

“I stayed a while; it was easy to eat as much as I could. I didn’t have to go foraging, it was just there, amazing.”

“This is what is happening for us Winni. The ‘Beings’ are leaving food in our little garden,” I stated.

“Oh, they like to feed the animals and birds,” she exclaimed.

“Eventually my leg got better, it must have been a magic stick, that is all I can think it could have been......a magic stick.”

“So, what happened then?” questioned another mouse.

“When my leg was completely better, I flew again from one bed to another, just over there. A very nice house I must say. It had dry clean grass and some food there too. I knew this was where I would stay."

"So here you are Winni," I said. "We love having you near us. It is good to know you are all better."

"Oh yes," she did the highest kick to the side she could. "Yes, all better, thank goodness for the magic stick."

"And the 'Beings," I added.

"Ohhhh most certainly, most certainly. I would not be here now if it wasn't for them."

"Winni?" said a little voice.

Winni turned round and noted the little mouse who had asked a question earlier. "Yes dear?"

"Winni, I don't have a name," she said in a small sad voice "Could 'you' give me one please?"

"Mmmm," thought Winni. "What about Magic? I think that might suit you quite well."

A big grin came on the small mouse's face, she looked so happy. Magic scurried away and we could hear her telling her family "Guess what?

Winni has given me my name....I'm called Magic."

"Wow," came the reply. "That's special."

Winni smiled and closed her eyes, she was delighted to be of assistance.

"Hey Winni, before you go to bed...... Do you know why the 'Beings' are spending more time in the space beyond our gardens? The stories of our ancestors do not mention such a peculiar thing," I anticipated excitedly her answer.

"As you already know Salta, I was taken in by the 'Beings when I hurt my leg. They were very kind to me but didn't communicate in squeak's, cough's, snuffles and click's, they had big open sounds. Round and wholesome with various pitch and vibrations," she explained.

"I learnt to understand their mood, and sense the feeling and thought behind their communication. It took some time but I understand their speech."

"So, do you know," Dearest and I both asked together...

"Yes" she replied with a mysterious tone. "But my story, will have to wait. I am sure we are all very tired now?"

We all agreed it was time for bed, and said we would gather in the same place during the next darkness to learn Why?

WE LEARNT……WHY?

During the next darkness when all our work was finished, we hurried about and gathered all our friends and relatives together. Just in the distance was Buffer pretending to sleep, so he really did want to know, and tucked up under a leaf were Coci and Neliday. I'm glad they came to find out too.

Winni was so proud to be centre of attention, and to actually have something important to say. So, she put on her best voice and began explaining the unusual behavior of the 'Beings'.

"I live in a house that the 'Beings' built for me. I like to stay close by because as I have already told you, two Great Suns ago they were very caring and looked after me so well." We pleaded with Winni to get on with the reason we were all gathered.

"Alright, alright," she smiled. "Do you remember the Great Sun's warmth came extra early?"

Yes, we all nodded in anticipation…

"That's when it started," she said. We all huddled closer.

"The 'Beings' have been told by their leader to stay at home, there is a germ called Cor-O-Na that is spreading all around and could kill them!" she expressed. Everyone exclaimed, and there was a mass of squeaking, moving around, sniffing and nodding to each other.

Winni raised one front paw to silence us. "Some are lucky to have their own gardens; some have been unable to breath and travel in the fresh air. It is a very sad time. The 'Beings' are not able to visit their friends and families, for fear of spreading Cor-O-Na." We felt great sadness, how could this happen? Not to see the mice we loved? We were in distress at the thought.

"How do you know this?" cried Kes.

Winni smiled "I know because I have heard the 'Beings' talk. The Great Sun has warmed the light and the darkness so much, the 'Beings' have stayed out in the dark. They stay and watch dancing lights in a cave, that gives out heat. And," she stopped talking to make sure we were all listening......." Mr. Toad did spy them during one darkness. He understands them too"

"Uggh, Mr. Toad," a mouse mumbled.

"He rustled some dry leaves and … was … found!" We all stared at her. "They crept over to him with a light as bright as the Great Sun," ... Winni then paused for a greater thrill, and we all held our breath... "But thankfully didn't harm him." We all sighed together in relief.

"Winni, you eat toads, don't you?" asked Little Lychee.

"Oh, Lychee, I try not to."

“Mr. Toad will eat you Lych,” taunted Cody.

“No he won't, I can run very fast,” replied Little Lychee, and we all squeaked and squirmed around just thinking of Mr. Toad.

“Come on everyone, shall I tell you some more?” Winni didn’t want to stop her important job of informing the mice of the germ. (Have you noticed reader? How Winni’s stories always get side-tracked?)

“YES,” we all shouted and settled down again.

“Some ‘Beings’ are eating too much, some are drinking the merry water’s, some have harmed each other and many, many have died from this Cor-O-Na germ, or the effects of it in different ways. It has been a dreadful time for them all.

“They have not even been able to dance, play or learn together.”

“No dancing!” we cried. We looked at each other, how can this be?... We loved dancing!

“This is still happening I tell you. Many are not able to find food, they have to wait to be given it by others, and because they cannot go out, they are becoming poorly in their mind and have great unrest deep in their soul." Winni explained.

"There have been some good things though. Have you noticed how quiet it has been?" she asked.

We sat and thought... "Yes," said Cody. "I haven't heard any rumbling or felt any vibration's deep in the ground."

"Oh yes," admitted Rapunz . "Where have all the Beasts with the shiny eyes gone?" He opened his eyes as wide as he could.

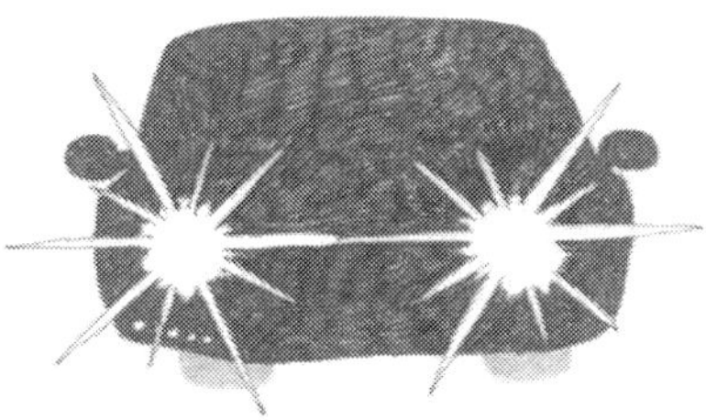

"Exactly," said Winni. "I even managed to cross the hard, dark surface without any fear."

We all looked at her in surprise!

“And just for the sheer joy of it, I wiggled-my-bottom as I went,” she chuckled.

We all laughed and tried to imagine Winni doing this.

“Because there haven’t been any of these beasts about, roaring along the hard-dark surface the air has been cleaner.”

The air was sniffed and admitted that this was true.

“And there haven't been any non-flappy birds in the sky either,” cried Kes, flapping his arms as best as he could. We all agreed, but it had taken Winni mentioning these things, for us to realise that this was so.

“Within the ‘Beings’ small family groups, they have become closer, spending special time with each other, they probably wouldn’t have done normally. Cupboards have been cleaned and jobs completed that have been waiting around. Then there’s the Great Sun. It has shone brightly and warm, so those that have been able to be out in their spaces beyond our gardens, have done so.”

"Mmmm," we all understood and nodded in unison.

"Mrs. Robin played her part too," Winni sighed. There were questioning looks all round. "Salta, your 'Beings' made friends with Mrs. Robin. She became very close to one of them. Usually sitting so high in that tree," Winni pointed up, "singing so loudly, doesn't she?"

Yes, we agreed. Some even rubbed their ears. "Well, she would sit very close and sing in a very quiet voice of joy and hope. She became a very comforting presence."

"So that's why we have seen them so much, they have had time to sit and be with us," holding my paws out expressing my understanding.

"Yes," agreed Winni.

"Now we know why, thank you Winni," they all chorused together.

"I hope they get better soon, it's not nice to be poorly," said Little Lychee.

"No," agreed Winni with a sad slow shake of her head. She then looked up and sensed the coming of the Great Sun. "It's time for us to be going to bed. I'm sure there will be more stories to tell, as the Cor-O-Na germ has not finished spreading and causing havoc, on the lives of the 'Beings'."

The mice were very thankful to Winni and fussed about, thanking her and saying their farewell's.

Winni was pleased to be of assistance, and said if there was any other time, they needed help, to just come-a-knocking.

"Would you like to join us for some meal worms Winni?" I asked.

"Ooh, I'll call in next time I'm passing, but I cannot eat the dry meal worms, or not too many, as they are not good for my bones. They are very yummy I know, but I have to be good," she winked.

As she turned to head home Rapunz called, "Hey Winni, we all know where our names come from, but we don't know about yours."

"Ah," smiled Winni, "the Beings gave me my name. I'm named after a place called Winnipeg." She shrugged her shoulders and said, "but I don't know where that is".

And so, the darkness turned to light and Winni snuggled into her home. We and the rest of the mice went back to our own homes and gardens, knowing and understanding the reason we were seeing the 'Beings' so often. Why they had their concerns and fears. We hoped all would be well soon.

THE BIRDS

Before I leave you, I will introduce you to some of the birds I have already mentioned that live near us, as we do share the same space and food. They are funny things; they can dart around as quick as us, but they can fly! Here and there they flit, to tops of trees, using them as look out points, singing a happy tune or warning each other of dangers.

Mr. and Mrs. Sparrow: They are very weary of everything. As I have said it took us both some time to get used to each other. They were very nervous and would fly off at the slightest breeze or movement, but eventually we could eat side by side.

“My name’s Salta, what's yours?”

“We are Mr. and Mrs. Passer,” they both said at the very same time, then picked up a morsel of food, and flew off again.

They love to gather in groups, play tag, and all shout very loudly together. Often, we think they are arguing, but they are just happy to be together. I asked them why they don’t sing like the other birds, “We prefer to talk, talk, talk, talk to each other,” was their reply, “we can get so much more out of a conversation than just singing.”

Do you know the other day I saw one being very cheeky, it plucked some feathers from Columbia the pigeon for her nest, I didn’t hear her ask either!

I enjoy watching them jig around in the dust, they say it's very good for them.

“We like to look after our feathers. Stroking them with our beaks brings oil to the surface. It’s good for them, but in the hot weather we might make too much, so we have a dust bath. Too much oil makes it difficult to fly," they told me.

Mrs. or is it Mr. Robin? I cannot tell which, has a lovely voice, and can sing very loud, or softly. Winni the hedgehog heard from the 'Beings' that they both have bright red front feathers and the perfect yellow eye liner. They sing about their lovely Orange tummies, and are amused that the 'Beings had no word for this colour.

"I have an orange tum,
though some may think it's red.
In days of old there was no word,
So, red it was, they said!"

Eventually we got to know her... Yes, she is female, and her name is Ruby. Do you know?... Ruby says that 'Beings' believe Robins to be a sign

that a loved one who has passed, is nearby, and looking out for them. She finds this a very important job to let them know all is well. She sees it in their faces that they are happy to see her.

“I am a bit lazy though,” she explained one time.

“Oh, why’s that?” I asked.

“I like to wait for ‘Beings’ to work on the land. I sit and wait for them to dig up worms for me, ha ha,” she twittered. “I’ll sometimes sit on the thing they are using, and sing a quiet song...... “Juicy worms come to me, juicy worms come to me.”

“How do I tell you apart from Mr. Robin?” I asked.

“This is my garden, and my garden only!” She exclaimed, “You will only see me here!” Ruby then calmed herself and smiled, "But every Robin has a unique coloured tummy. We are all different.”

Ruby is a beautiful bird but she does have a temper, and she cannot share! She is not nice to a Dunnock bird called Prunella, who, if eating quite quietly by herself, Ruby will come along and attack her and make her squeak. Poor Pru.

Pru and her friends most of the time, feed on their own and a little apart from each other. They seem to be at the bottom of the food chain and gather up the left-overs from the ground. They are quiet and actually were the first we met under our Acer.

We learnt again from Winni, that they were the reason why the meal worms came into our garden. The 'Beings' felt sorry for them and found what they thought was a secret place for them to feed...that was until Dearest and I moved in Ha ha.

So Pru and her two friends were provided for, they took the opportunity and fed well from our garden, and we ate with them too.

She made us laugh one time. In the space beyond our garden where the 'Beings' are, there are two very large shiny objects. I once went past it and so did another mouse at the side of me! It was a bit scary at first but Winni explained it was called a mirror, and it was me, me I could see. Amazing…... I could look at my whiskers, nose and mouth.....teeth, stick my tongue out at myself, so funny. But Pru just couldn't understand. She stood there for ages pecking at the mirror, walking this way and back again. Tap, tap tap... tap, tap,tap.

"HEY PRU, THAT'S YOU!" I called, but she just carried on. Eventually I think she got fed up trying to make friends and left... only to repeat again the next time she passed.

There are the Blackbirds. Meru is the male bird. He is a fine bird and will let all the other birds, and us know when there is a cat about. He Chooks..." Cat, cat, cat, C. A. T." We all take cover until he gives the all clear or one of the 'Beings' comes and shoo's the cat away.

Meru and his wife have their own pile of food including meal worms but they come and share ours too. You should see how many they can get in their beaks at any one time! I counted at least twelve maybe more when they were feeding their young! Like Ruby, Meru has the perfect eye liner that makes him look very handsome too. I might add that he and his wife make sure their family is fed well, and will fend off the greedy Starlings until they have taken what they need.

It is believed by all animals that if a Blackbirds nest is near to your own house, it is a sign of good luck.

Now I must mention those greedy Starlings. They all come down together and create a great fuss, the other birds don't get a chance. The food is quickly taken, eaten and even squabbled over within their own families. Such a noise, but so confident, probably because

they all work together as one unit. I never got to know any of their names, they didn't seem very friendly and looked very STERN all the time.

Pelia the Collared Dove visits too, she sits and picks at her food very daintily, she is very entertaining to watch. Once she landed on the stick with all the food hanging on it, but she couldn't get to it, she had to go on the flat piece sticking out. She was ages wondering how to reach it, she had done it before but maybe had forgotten! Should she go this way or that way? How was she to

get there? Eventually she jumped down and ate her fill.

Funnily enough Pelia took to liking herself in the mirror too. She would walk around a magnolia tree as if she was just out for a stroll, then see her reflection and run so fast up to it, as if to shoo it away. There she would stand and stare, then repeat the process again, and again. It didn't take her too long to figure out that there wasn't another. Or maybe she just got fed up. She is quite a pretty bird though, so I understand her using the mirror.

Columbia the Wood Pigeon is a bit bigger than Pelia, and she hasn't got the black ring around her neck. But oh dear, Columbia poos in her own food, why does she do that?

Ace the Sparrowhawk comes often and we all know to hide.

He sits at the top of a big tree and waits and waits.

He waits for some poor thing to make a move, to get fed up of hiding, and takes them away and eats them for dinner. One time he came and Columbia was sat in the food on the big stick. I have never seen her sit so very still; she did not move at-all. Even when Ace had flown off in a huff, she still sat motionless for quite a while.

Later, she said her heart was beating so very fast and loud, she thought we all might have heard it!

Finally, thank goodness those seagulls called Lari never land, they are so big they just fly over in groups looking for something, I know not what. I've never met one but they call out to each other “La-ri, La-ri, La-ri” How do they know who to answer to?

AS TIME PASSED

Time and life seem to pass by so quickly when you think back. So much happens, then it all seems to bunch together, and we wonder, was it then or did it happen then?

I am so happy I have been able to tell you of my friends and family, it is so important that even you reader, talk and tell stories of happenings, whether they are sad or happy. Experiences make us what we are, and we learn so much.

After the story was told to us by Winni we all went back to our regular comings and goings but we were now aware of the sadness and desperate feelings of the 'Beings'. We saw them every time the Great Sun appeared and we knew. If it hadn't had been for the germ, they may not have noticed the plight of Prunella and her few friends. The food wouldn't have been put in this garden of ours, but then we wouldn't have come here. We smelt the mealworms, we knew this was a good place for us to be and have our babies. Things happen for a reason, we might not know or see the reasons at first, but they will unfurl before us and explain themselves.

You now may like to follow our story a little more...

My babies soon grew. At first they cried a lot and were very wrinkly and pink, but after a short time they became soft and fuzzy, lovely to stroke, and they didn't cry as much thank goodness. Excitement, excitement when they opened their eyes and saw Dearest and myself for the first time. We were both busy, busy,

busy. I had to keep myself fed well, so I could feed them.

Soon it was time for my babies to venture out. The garden was so safe I didn't mind them wandering around on their own. They would climb through a Jasmine bush and land on the little garden under the Acer.

When my babies left me, it was a sad moment, I hoped they too would find a garden such as ours. We said our goodbye's and they disappeared into the Jasmine. Oh, do not worry... I was readying myself to have more babies so I wouldn't miss them too much, a mother's work is never done!

Dearest had made me a new annex in the Jasmine, a superb mouse-in-waiting place. A place I could go to get away from all the hustle and bustle and comings and goings of him, and dare I say it, relatives! I had many, many babies throughout the time of the Great Sun. I was kept very busy indeed, as my next pregnancy produced 7 just as Neliday had predicted!

Oh, my goodness what a lot, but with the help of Dearest all was well. They all survived to go out and make a life for themselves and, I hope have lots of adventures.

Mr. and Mrs. Sparrow, had some baby chicks. Mrs. Sparrow laid some eggs in the nest that Mr. Sparrow had built, which was very nice of him, wasn't it? She says she lost some of her feathers on her tummy so she could incubate her eggs better. She has to keep them warm so the baby birds develop inside.

Once hatched and later have their own feathers, they can soon fly away. Mr. Sparrow says it's such hard work keeping them fed until they can find their own food, but they enjoy doing this. The fledglings, that's what they are called, stand and vibrate their wings so fast when they want to be fed, even when they are stood next to food!

Sometimes other Sparrows who haven't been able to have babies feed them too which is a great help.

Mrs. Robin, well she continued to keep her eye on the female 'Being' and sing very

quietly and close to her. I'm not sure if Ruby had any babies, as baby Robins look so much like baby Sparrows to me, and, she didn't let me know! I think she likes to keep us guessing.

Pru had chicks too but we never seemed to have time to talk. She and her family kept to themselves and I believe were very thankful of the special place in our garden to feed.

Meru and his wife had two chicks. We only saw them when they had left their nest and were calling for food. They often came to our little garden and were fed mealworms one after the other. They seemed to have their mouths open all the time! Meru was very patient and continued to feed them without a complaint. Where was Mrs. Blackbird? Why wasn't she helping? In-between mouthfuls Meru told me she had been caught by a cat and he had had to look after his chicks by himself. They had met before the last Great Sun. It was very sad but he had the chicks to think about which kept him very busy. Later he would find "a new Mrs."

The Starling group grew and grew in numbers throughout the time of the Great Sun. Always first down to the food on the big stick. Always arguing within their family, Oh what a noise!

Pelia tried to make a nest in the Wisteria. It looked very flimsy to me, and I'm afraid it didn't support her eggs. Winni later told me the 'Beings' had bought her a house too. It looked very posh to me, very high on a big stick as thick as a tree with the house on top of it. Pelia said "No, I cannot use that house, I like to be in the open air. I'll take a look but no, I will not use it."

Oh dear, Ace took Columbia. There was such a commotion. Ace had appeared and all the little birds had taken cover. Columbia takes too long to take to flight, and she was caught by Ace, and we never saw her again!

Dear Winni had six babies. I went to visit as there was no sign of Mr. Hedgehog. “Oh no,” said Winni. “He won't stick around, gone orf to explore. I won't see him again.” Her babies were so sweet. Their spines had just appeared and were soft to touch. Winni is thankful the spines are under the skin when they are born, as you can imagine!

They took a little longer than mine to go out of their house for the first time. Winni was very protective and they stayed by her side. One she calls Junior still lives with her, and seems to have no intention of moving out. Winni says he may set up a little nest right next door to her.

The weather is now turning. I can feel it. The sky looks different, and it’s raining more. We are not seeing the ‘Beings’ in the spaces beyond our gardens. They are staying away, keeping warm in their houses. There's still plenty of food arriving for both us and the birds, but it appears and that's it.

We are getting ready for the cold, for the time when our bodies slow down and we sleep longer than usual. We don't hibernate (go to sleep during the cold weather) like Winni, but we gather in our holes and keep warm. Our food storage is full to overflowing so we have no reason really to go out. It may even snow I have been told. I wonder if I will see snow?

Winni has become pregnant again but it is a bit late and will be too cold for her to have babies, so she has put them 'on hold' until the next Great Sun, which is quite amazing isn't it? A bit like Coci and Nelliday.

Cody and Little Lychee, you may wonder... all of their competitiveness ended with them falling in love and having some babies together. I knew it, I am such a romantic mouse. Poor Little Lychee had a bother with her first pregnancy. A strange mouse, one not seen in our area before came by. Lychee knew she was newly pregnant and hoped all would be well as if we smell the urine of a strange male, we can lose our babies before they take hold inside us. But Lychee was lucky and she was gratefully relieved that her natural body worked for her. As females we are able to block our sense of smell at such times, incredible, eh?

Before Winni took to her bed for the Long Darkness she told me the that the Cor-O-Na germ was still out there, and the 'Beings' were still dying. As it was colder, they were told to stay home for a longer time. I hope all will be well by the next Great Sun as I will not be here, but I'll be thinking of you.

NATURE NOTES

(By Salta)

Hi this is Salta, thank you for reading my story. I would like to tell you now, about us, the Wood Mouse. Our name in Latin (Scientific name) is quite unusual *Apodemus sylvaticus.* It's very long and doesn't seem to say mouse at all does it?!

We are found in Europe and Northwest Africa, and measure about 90mm in length from our nose to the tip of our tail, and can weigh up to 23g. We are common, common, common. I hate being common, but there are so many of us, so many babies. I love having babies. I might add we do have big eyes and ears, lovely golden-brown shiny fur and a pale tummy (unless you are called Rapunz!).

It takes 25-26 light times for babies to grow in my tummy, which doesn't sound long, but its long enough for me when there can be between 4 and 8 bouncing around in there! Although I did only have 3 for my first litter. Babies can be born during the Long Darkness if there's lots of food about, and the weather isn't too cold. The nests are lined with leaves, moss and grass and my specialty... rose petals.

We live in forests, grasslands, farmers' fields and even your garden, but seek out wooded areas and lots of cover for the Long Darkness, maybe even finding a building to live in. If it gets very, very cold, we slow down. Our body temperature lowers so energy is saved by not having to keep us warm, though we do not hibernate fully. (Hibernation is when some animals go to sleep during the cold Long Darkness, and wake up refreshed when the new flowers appear – like Winni does)

There are quite a few of us in our set of tunnels, all busy, busy, passing each other and saying Hi, and maybe explaining where the best spot is for food. We have very sensitive whiskers that we use to let us know the different surfaces and textures we find, and they tell us what the temperature is outside. The tunnel system has 2 open entrances and others are blocked with stones, leaves or sticks. These are private, so don't tell! Oh, we like to climb and jump too, especially to get those berries that are up high. Mrs. Robin gets a surprise sometimes....

Our favourite foods are; seeds from many trees including Oak, Ash, Lime, Hawthorn, Sycamore, and fruits such as lovely juicy berries, fungi and roots. Having a sharp sense of smell enables us to hunt out freshly sown seeds, not making much mess at all we just dig straight down to the seed... which doesn't make us very popular with some 'Beings'. We might even eat a snail or two and of course the mealworms and seeds left out for the garden birds. Food will be taken back to our nests for storage, never eating too much, always saving some. As you already know I was out and about during the time of the Great Sun, this was because I was feeding my babies, they want to drink so much milk... to grow up big and strong.

I am a romantic mouse I love Dearest with all my heart and it is true, mice do serenade each other with love songs.

This is the end of my story, but I see the Author has written some questions for you of which you will not find all the answers to in this book.

Bless you all.

Love Salta

NATURE QUESTIONS

1. What is the Scientific name of the Ladybird?

2. Why does the ladybird cry "Find Ann" when it flies off?

3. What is the yellow flower called Brassica used for?

4. What sort of flower is Madam Pierre, and what does it smell like?

5. How far can a mouse travel when it is foraging for food?

6. Look up some more Scientific names for the animals in this book?

7. What sort of nest does a Dove make?

8. Why do birds wash in the soil?

9. Why do Toads have warts?

10. Do Toads hibernate? If so, where?

11. Where do mice live?

12. Do mice hibernate?

13. How does a mouse find its way home?

14. How far can a Kestrel see?

15. Why do stars twinkle?

16. What are comets?

17. What do you think the Big Buzzy thing is? And can you find out how many beats per second its wings move?

18. Can you find out when the word Orange was first used in British history?

ADDITIONAL FACTS

(From The Author)

- Mice and hedgehogs are colour blind (blue/green) and so cannot see all the different colours we can. (Hedgehogs can only see creams and browns)

- Mice sadly only live for one year, and most often will not see two Great Suns.

- The action of termination of babies due to the scent of a strange male is called the 'Bruce effect'

- It is very rare for a Kestrel to drop its prey because, if the captured animal wriggles - the talons naturally get tighter.

- The bumble bee you read of is a Queen Bee who slept over the Winter in a small hole in the ground. Once awake she lay her eggs maybe in an abandoned mouse nest or a small cavity. When her first born emerge as an adult, she stops her daily task of foraging and leaves it to the workers.

- This is my first time for drawing mice and birds – so those in the 'know' please forgive any inaccuracies.

- There is a reason behind all the names of the animals in this story. The only one I haven't explained is Cody. The name is very similar to someone my friends and I met in the Castro district of San Francisco, and had a lovely memorable evening together.

ACKNOWLEDGEMENTS

I would like to give thanks to the following people:

To Mumsie and Pa who continue to give the only encouragement parents can – the best, and to my Sister, I could not wish for more.

To Gary, my partner, for being him. Such a laid-back person he is horizontal. He gives continuous support for any project I am doing. Never complains, and even will have sandwiches for Sunday dinner.

For my readers, who advised with optimism: Karen and Holly Wright, June Herrick, Eileen Smith, Carol Frankish.

Special thanks go to Holly for drawing the logo and letting me use it. Holly Cottage Books was born.

Printed in Great Britain
by Amazon

77085343R00078